Pins and Needles

Rob Drummond

T0284299

methuen | drama

LONDON • NEW YORK • OXFORD • NEW DELHI • SYDNEY

METHUEN DRAMA
Bloomsbury Publishing Plc
50 Bedford Square, London, WC1B 3DP, UK
1385 Broadway, New York, NY 10018, USA
29 Earlsfort Terrace, Dublin 2, Ireland

BLOOMSBURY, METHUEN DRAMA and the Methuen
Drama logo are trademarks of Bloomsbury Publishing Plc

First published in Great Britain 2024

A catalogue record for this book is available from the British Library.

A catalog record for this book is available from the Library of Congress.

ISBN: PB: 978-1-3505-3508-4
ePDF: 978-1-3505-3509-1
eBook: 978-1-3505-3510-7

Series: Modern Plays

Typeset by Mark Heslington Ltd, Scarborough, North Yorkshire

To find out more about our authors and books visit
www.bloomsbury.com and sign up for our newsletters.

Kiln Theatre presents

CAUTION: Contains Truth, Lies & Mis-information. You decide.

Pins and Needles

By Rob Drummond

Directed by Amit Sharma

CAST

Mary
Vivienne Acheampong

Edward Jenner
Richard Cant

Rob
Gavi Singh Chera

Robert
Brian Vernel

CREATIVE TEAM

Writer
Rob Drummond

Director
Amit Sharma

Designer
Frankie Bradshaw

Lighting Designer
Rory Beaton

Sound Designer
Jasmin Kent Rodgman

Casting Director
Amy Ball CDG

Voice and Dialect Coach
Danièle Lydon

Kiln-Mackintosh Resident Assistant Director
Imy Wyatt Corner

Linbury Associate Designer
Finlay Jenner

Costume Supervisor
Lisa Aitken

Wig Supervisor
Suzanne Scotcher

PRODUCTION TEAM

Production Manager
Andy Reader

Company Stage Manager
Katie Bachtler

Deputy Stage Manager
Odette Robertson

Assistant Stage Manager (Book Cover)
Stella Wang

Technician
Jahmal Swaby

Tech Swing
Dominique Nesbeth

Wardrobe Manager
Céline Castillon

Wigs, Hair and Make-Up Manager
Milica Rosellini

Production Electrician
Paul Salmon

Lighting Programmer
Jack Ryan

Production Sound Engineer
Richard Bell

Production Carpenter
Ben Dackerman

Set built by
Footprint Scenery
Kiln Theatre Workshop

BIOGRAPHIES

CAST

VIVIENNE ACHEAMPONG
MARY

Theatre credits include: *Is God Is* (Royal Court); *Nassim* (Bush Theatre); *City of Glass* (Lyric Hammersmith/HOME Manchester); *Monster Raving Loony* (Soho Theatre); *Rainbow Class*(Assembly Hall, Edinburgh Fringe Festival); *Elegies for Angela, Punks & Raging Queens* (Criterion Theatre); *The Curious Incident of the Dog in the Night-Time* (Gielgud Theatre) and*Julius Caesar* (Donmar Warehouse/ St Ann's Warehouse).

Film credits include: *Jackdaw* and *The Witches*.

Television credits include: *The Sandman, Everything Now, Ellie & Natasia, The One, The Emily Atack Show, The Other One, Famalam, Death in Paradise, Turn Up Charlie, We the Jury*and *The Aliens*.

RICHARD CANT
EDWARD JENNER

For Kiln: *Handbagged* and *Wife*.

Theatre credits include: *Chariots of Fire, Talent* (Sheffield Theatres); *What it Means* (The Lot at Wilton's Music Hall); *The Vortex* (Chichester Festival Theatre); *Orlando* (MGC at the Garrick Theatre); *The Normal Heart, Mr Gum and the Dancing Bear* (National Theatre); *After Edward, Edward the Second* (Shakespeare's Globe); *Maydays, Henry VI – Rebellion and Wars of the Roses* (Royal Shakespeare Company); *Saint Joan* (Donmar Warehouse); *My Night with Reg* (Donmar Warehouse/Apollo

Theatre); *Medea* (Almeida Theatre); *The Trial* (Young Vic); *War Horse* (New London Theatre) and *Salome* (Headlong).

Television credits include: *Doctor Who, Mapp & Lucia, The Crown, It's a Sin, Silent Witness, Taboo, Outlander, Bleak House* and *The Way We Live Now*.

Film credits include: *Take Care, My Policeman, Mary Queen of Scots* and *Stan and Ollie*.

GAVI SINGH CHERA
ROB

Theatre credits include: *Our Generation* (National Theatre/Chichester Festival Theatre); *Behind the Beautiful Forevers* (National Theatre); *Pygmalion* (Headlong); *The Cherry Orchard* (Yard Theatre/HOME Theatre); *Duck, 1922: The Waste Land* (Jermyn Street Theatre); as well as numerous West End productions whilst a member of the National Youth Theatre REP Company, including *Wuthering Heights, Consensual* and *The Merchant of Venice*.

Television credits include: *The Lord of the Rings: The Rings of Power, The Undeclared War, The Lazarus Project* and *Vera*.

Film credits include: *Blitz, Kavita and Teresa* and short film *Temple* – for which he was nominated for Best Actor in the British Short Film Awards.

BRIAN VERNEL
ROBERT

Theatre credits include: *Mary* (Hampstead Theatre); *Stories, Certain Young Men – Queer Theatre* (National Theatre); *Instructions for Correct Assembly* (Royal Court); *The Seagull* (Lyric Hammersmith);

Barbarians, *Future Conditional* (Young Vic); *Takin' Over the Asylum* (Royal Lyceum/ Citizens Theatre); *The Static*, *Blackout* (Corby Cube) and *Four Parts Broken* (National Theatre of Scotland/Traverse Theatre/Òran Mór).

Television credits include: *Shardlake*, *Slow Horses*, *Gangs of London*, *Collateral*, *The Tunnel*, *Doctor Who*, *The Missing 2*, *The Last Kingdom*, *The Casual Vacancy*, *Grantchester*, *Prey* and *The Field of Blood*.

Film credits include: *Kill*, *Dunkirk*, *Papillon*, *Star Wars: The Force Awakens*, *Winter Song*, *Offender* and *Let Us Prey*.

CREATIVE TEAM

ROB DRUMMOND
WRITER

Rob Drummond is an award-winning playwright and performer who has worked with the most prestigious theatres in the UK and as an associate artist at the Traverse Theatre.

Playwrighting credits include: *Roald Dahl's The Wonderful Story of Henry Sugar* (Perth Theatre/Macrobert Arts Centre/ Eden Court Theatre); *Milkshake*, *The Mack*, *Eulogy* (Òran Mór/Traverse Theatre); *Flesh* (National Theatre Connections); *Our Fathers* (Traverse Theatre/Tron Theatre/Scottish Tour); *Grain in the Blood* (Traverse Theatre/Tron Theatre); *In Fidelity* (HighTide/Traverse Theatre); *Bullet Catch* (Brits Off Broadway 59East59/International Tour/Traverse Theatre – Herald Angel Award and Total Theatre Award); *Quiz Show* (Traverse Theatre/National Theatre of Scotland – CATS Award for Best New Play); *Pleading, Top Table, Rolls in Their Pockets* (Òran Mór – A Play, A Pie and A Pint); *The Majority* (National Theatre); *The Broons* (Scottish Tour); *In Uncanny Valley* (Edinburgh International Science Festival/Borderline Theatre – CATS Award, Best Production for Children and Young People); *Dear Scotland* (National Theatre of Scotland); *The Riot of Spring* (The Arches Theatre, Glasgow); *Rob Drummond: Wrestling* (The Arches – Vital Spark Award);

Mr Write (NTS, Tron Theatre – CATS Award, Best Production for Children and Young People); *Hunter* (NTS/Frantic Assembly); *Allotment* (Govan Shopping Centre) and *Sixteen* (Arches Theatre Festival).

For television his work includes: *McDonald and Dodds.*

AMIT SHARMA
DIRECTOR

Amit Sharma is an international award-winning director of theatre and television. Before joining the Kiln Theatre as Associate Director and then Artistic Director, he was Deputy Artistic Director of Birmingham Rep, Associate Artistic Director at the Royal Exchange, Manchester, and Associate Director at Graeae Theatre Company where his journey into theatre began. Sharma directed the critically acclaimed and sell-out run of *Retrograde* at the Kiln; and has also directed two productions at the National Theatre – *The Solid Life of Sugar Water* (Graeae Theatre Company/Theatre Royal Plymouth co-production) and *The Boy with Two Hearts* (also Wales Millennium Centre). He also co-directed *Prometheus Awakes*, one of the largest outdoor productions featuring Deaf and disabled artists as part of the London 2012 Cultural Olympiad (Graeae Theatre Company/Greenwich+Docklands International Festival/Stockton International Riverside Festival/La Fura Dels Baus); and *Aruna and The Raging Sun* in Chennai, India as part of UK/India Year of Culture 2017. Sharma is a BAFTA-nominated director for his two films which were part of the *Criptales* season on BBC and BBC America. He also co-directed the award-winning BBC and Netflix television drama *Then Barbara Met Alan* (Best Single Drama, 2023 Broadcast Awards). He began his training at Graeae Theatre Company with *Missing Piece 1*. His other theatre credits include *One Under* (Graeae Theatre Company/Theatre Royal Plymouth), *Cosmic Scallies* (Graeae Theatre Company/Royal Exchange Theatre) and *Iron Man* (Graeae Theatre Company/

International Tour). His other television work includes *Hamish* and *Thunderbox*.

FRANKIE BRADSHAW
DESIGNER

For Kiln: *Retrograde.*

Theatre credits include: *Dear Octopus* (Lyttelton, National Theatre); *Blues for an Alabama Sky* (National Theatre – Olivier Award nomination, Best Costume Design); *Hamlet* (National Theatre/UK Tour); *Macbeth* (Wessex Grove/Shakespeare Theatre Company, Washington); *Sweat* (Donmar Warehouse/Gielgud Theatre); *Clyde's, Assembly* (Donmar Warehouse); *Mad House* (Ambassadors Theatre); *Never Have I Ever, Local Hero, The Long Song* (Chichester Festival Theatre); *Starter For Ten* (Bristol Old Vic); *Unexpected Twist, Two Trains Running* (Royal & Derngate Theatre); *House of Ife* (Bush Theatre); *We Started to Sing* (Arcola Theatre); *Beautiful: The Carole King Musical* (Leicester Curve/UK Tour); *A Christmas Carol, Beauty and the Beast* (Rose Theatre, Kingston); *The Lemon Table* (MGC/Wiltshire Creative); *Piaf, Skellig* (Nottingham Playhouse); *Cinderella* (Lyric Hammersmith); *A Christmas Carol* (Theatre Clwyd); *Napoli Brooklyn* (UK Tour/Park Theatre); *Trying it On* (UK Tour/Royal Shakespeare Company/Royal Court); *Kiss Me Kate, Jerusalem, Nesting, Robin Hood* (Watermill Theatre); *Cookies* (Theatre Royal Haymarket); *On the Exhale* (Traverse) and *Hansel* (Salisbury Playhouse).

Opera designs include: *ITCH* (World Premiere Opera Holland Park); *Macbeth, Idomeneo* and *Elizabetta* (English Touring Opera).

Dance designs include: *Pinocchio* (Northern Ballet).

Production and costume designs for film: *The Talent* (Second Name Productions).

RORY BEATON
LIGHTING DESIGNER

Rory Beaton recently won the Broadway World Award for Best Lighting Design for his work on *The Lord of the Rings* which is now playing in the US and New Zealand. He was also nominated for the 2024 WhatsOnStage Award for his work on *The Time Traveller's Wife* and a Knight of Illumination Award for his work on *Così fan Tutte* at Opera Holland Park.

Theatre credits include: *For Black Boys...* (Royal Court/Apollo Theatre/Garrick Theatre); *The Time Traveller's Wife Musical* (Apollo Theatre); *Death Drop: Back in the Habit, Instructions for a Teenage Armageddon* (Garrick Theatre); *Jews. In Their Own Words* (Royal Court); *The Merchant of Venice 1936* (Royal Shakespeare Company/Criterion Theatre/Trafalgar Theatre); *Wild About You* (Theatre Royal Drury Lane); *Your Lie in April* (Harold Pinter Theatre); *I Love You, You're Perfect, Now Change!* (London Coliseum); *Starter for Ten* (Bristol Old Vic); *Lovely Ugly City* (Almeida Theatre); *The Creakers* (Theatre Royal Plymouth/Southbank Centre); *Principles of Deception* (Royal & Derngate); *Unexpected Twist* (UK Tour); *The Jungle Book* (Chichester Festival Theatre); *Midsummer* (Mercury Theatre); *Half Empty Glasses, A Sudden Violent Burst of Rain, The Ultimate Pickle* (Paines Plough); *Spike* (UK Tour); *Edward II* (Cambridge Arts Theatre) and *Marx in London!* (Scottish Opera).

JASMIN KENT RODGMAN
SOUND DESIGNER

British-Malaysian Artist & Composer Jasmin Kent Rodgman brings together the contemporary classical, electronics and sound art worlds to create powerful soundscapes and musical identities.

Sound Designer credits include: *Julius Ceasar* (Royal Shakespeare Company); *Titus Andronicus* (Shakespeare's Globe); *Bindweed* (Mercury Theatre); *The EU Killed My Dad* (Jermyn Street Theatre); *Paradise Now* (Bush Theatre); *Brown Girls Do It Too* (Soho Theatre); *Dorian* (Reading Rep); *Nineteen Ways of Looking* (Chinese Arts Now); *At Home with the World* (Bagri Foundation) and *Culture Mile* (London Symphony Orchestra).

Composer credits include: *Prisoner C33* (BBC/Pioneer Productions); and *Nanjing* (feature film, with a live production at Bush Theatre, London and a new 2021 digital commission for Music Theatre Wales).

Composer and Sound Designer credits include: *Britannicus* (Lyric Hammersmith); *Red Ellen* (Northern Stage); *Missing Julie* (Theatre Clywd) and *Harm* (BBC Film).

AMY BALL CDG
CASTING DIRECTOR

For Kiln: *The Son* (also Duke of York's Theatre).

Theatre credits include: *Alma Mater, Cold War, Portia Coughlan, Women, Beware the Devil, "Daddy": A Melodrama, Albion, The Hunt, Shipwreck, Dance Nation, Boy* (Almeida Theatre); *Hamnet* (Royal Shakespeare Company); *Lyonesse, The Hills of California, Uncle Vanya, Who's Afraid of Virginia Woolf?* (Harold Pinter Theatre); *Jerusalem* (Apollo Theatre); *Leopoldstadt* (Wyndham's Theatre); *The Night of the Iguana* (Noël Coward Theatre); *Rosmersholm, The Pillowman* (Duke of York's Theatre); *The Moderate Soprano* (Hampstead Theatre/Duke of York's Theatre); *True West* (Vaudeville Theatre); *The Goat, or Who is Sylvia?* (Theatre Royal Haymarket); *Sweat* (Donmar Warehouse/Gielgud Theatre); *The Ferryman* (Royal Court/Bernard B. Jacobs Theatre/Gielgud Theatre); *The Birthday Party, Consent* (National Theatre/Harold Pinter Theatre); *Stories, Exit the King* (National Theatre); *Hangmen* (Royal Court/Wyndham's Theatre/Atlantic Theater Company); *Maryland, ear for eye, Girls & Boys, Cyprus Avenue* (Royal Court); *Berberian Sound Studio* (Donmar Warehouse); *White Noise, A Very Very Very Dark Matter* (Bridge Theatre) and *The Brothers Size* (Young Vic).

DANIÈLE LYDON
VOICE AND DIALECT COACH

Danièle Lydon has an MA in Voice from the Royal Central School of Speech.

Theatre credits include: *Kiss Me Kate* (The Barbican); *The Picture of Dorian Gray* (The Picture of Dorian Gray); *The Hills of California* (Harold Pinter Theatre); *Moulin Rouge* (Piccadilly Theatre); *The Mirror and the Light* (Gielgud Theatre); *The Lion King* (Lyceum Theatre); *Billy Elliot the Musical* (Victoria Palace/UK Tour); *Shrek the Musical* (UK Tour); *School of Rock* (Gillian Lynne Theatre); *The Twilight Zone* (Almeida Theatre); *Harry Potter and the Cursed Child* (Palace Theatre/World Tour); *The King and I* (London Palladium); *Fan Girls* (Lyric Hammersmith); *Hamnet* (RSC); *The Crucible* (The National) and *Just for One Day* (Old Vic).

Television credits include: *Flight 103, The House of the Dragon, The Sandman, The English and Top Boy.*

Film credits include: *Blue Jean, Death on the Nile, Downton Abbey: A New Era, A Dog's Way Home and Rogue One – A Star Wars Story.*

IMY WYATT CORNER
KILN-MACKINTOSH RESIDENT ASSISTANT DIRECTOR

Imy Wyatt Corner is Resident Assistant Director at Kiln Theatre. She trained on the Drama Directing MA at Bristol Old Vic Theatre School.

Directing credits include: *The Last One* (Arcola Theatre); *Passing* (Park Theatre); *Scarlet Sunday* (Omnibus Theatre); *Duck* (Arcola Theatre); *BEASTS* (Edinburgh Fringe); *A Midsummer Night's Dream* (The Grove DIY Skatepark); *Humane* (Pleasance Theatre); *Walk Swiftly & with Purpose* (North Wall Arts Centre/Theatre503); *Baby, What Blessings* (Theatre503/Bunker Theatre) and *Happy Yet?* (Edinburgh Fringe/International Theatre, Frankfurt).

Associate/Assistant Director credits include: *Private Lives* (Ambassadors Theatre); *Relatively Speaking* (Theatre Royal Bath/UK Tour); *The Dance of Death* (Theatre Royal Bath/UK Tour); *Love All* (Jermyn Street Theatre) and *The Straw Chair* (Finborough Theatre).

She was a Creative Associate at Jermyn Street Theatre 2022/3 and an Associate Artist at Arcola Theatre 2023/4.

FINLAY JENNER
LINBURY ASSOCIATE DESIGNER

Finlay Jenner is a performance designer and theatre maker from South London. He grew up in South London and trained in Fine Art at the University for the Creative Arts then went on to train in Theatre and Performance Design at Liverpool Institute for Performing Arts, graduating in 2023. He was made a 2023 recipient of The Linbury Prize and had his work exhibited at the National Theatre.

Finlay is particularly drawn to avant-garde and contemporary performance practices with a design process that thrives on playful collaboration and multidisciplinary experimentation. He works across various fields, including dance, opera and diverse forms of theatre.

Theatre credits include: *Mantelpeace* at the Young Vic as Set Designer, *Hedda Gabler* and *A Bright New Boise* at LAMDA as the Set & Costume Designer, *Dorothy* at the Institute of Contemporary Arts as Set Designer and *Rita Lynn* at The Turbine Theatre as Set & Lighting Designer. Finlay also works as an assistant designer at the Greek National Opera.

LISA AITKEN
COSTUME SUPERVISOR

Costume Supervisor credits include: *Rough Magic* (Splendid Productions/ Shakespeare's Globe); *The Syndicate* (Band of Gold Productions UK Tour); *The Human Body, Clyde's, Henry V, When Winston Went to War with the Wireless* (Donmar Warehouse); *The Odyssey, Pericles, Kerry Jackson* (National Theatre); *Cymbeline, Richard III, The Whip, The Provoked Wife* (Royal Shakespeare Company); *Local Hero* (Chichester Festival Theatre); *Antigone, Oliver Twist* (Regent's Park Open Air Theatre); *Fantastically Great Women Who Changed the World* (Kenny Wax Family Entertainment); *Blue/Orange, The Turn of the Screw, Charlotte & Theodore, Intimate Apparel* (Theatre Royal Bath Ustinov Studio); *My Cousin Rachel* (Theatre Royal Bath); *Home, I'm Darling* (Theatre by the

Lake); *Death of a Black Man* (Hampstead Theatre); *Caroline, or Change* (Hampstead Theatre/Playhouse Theatre); *Shipwreck, Vassa* (Almeida Theatre); *Sweat* (Gielgud Theatre); *Titanic, the Musical* (UK & International Tour); *Dealing with Clair* (Orange Tree Theatre); *The Rise and Fall of Little Voice* (Theatr Clwyd); *The Boy in the Striped Pyjamas* (Northern Ballet); *Babette's Feast* (The Print Room at the Coronet); *Othello* (Shakespeare's Globe Sam Wanamaker Playhouse) and *Opera for the Unknown Woman* (Fuel Theatre).

Associate Costume Supervisor credits include: *Burlesque the Musical* (Adarma Productions); *Henry VI: Rebellion, War of the Roses* (Royal Shakespeare Company); *Endeavour: Bear Grylls Live Arena Tour* (Stufish Productions) and *Ghost: The Musical* (UK Tour & Korean-language production, Seoul).

TV credits include: *Masked Singer, Masked Dancer, Peaky Blinders* and *The Gallows Pole*.

SUZANNE SCOTCHER
WIG SUPERVISOR

Wigs, Hair and Make-Up Supervisor credits include: *Tammy Faye, The Chair, The Secret Life of Bees, Macbeth* (Almedia Theatre); *School Girls, or, The African Mean Girls, Cinderella, Peter Pan* (Lyric Hammersmith); *Pillowman, Vanya* (Duke of York's Theatre); *The Human Body* (Donmar Warehouse); *Starter for 10* (Bristol Old Vic); *Mandela* (Young Vic); *One Man, Two Guvnors* (National Theatre/Adelphi Theatre/International Tour); *The Grapes of Wrath, Underdog, Dancing at Lughnasa, The Father and the Assassin, Phaedra, Much Ado About Nothing, Trouble in Mind, When We Have Sufficiently Tortured Each Other, Master Harold and the Boys, An Octoroon, Saint George and the Dragon, Common, Ugly Lies the Bone, wonder.land, The James Plays, Men Should Weep, Never So Good, Home* (National Theatre) and *Bach & Sons* (Bridge Theatre).

Wigs, Hair and Make-Up Designer credits include: *Jitney* (Old Vic); *The Chairs* (Almeida Theatre); *Second Woman* and *Passing Strange* (Young Vic).

"Kiln Theatre has revitalised the cultural life of Brent and brings world-class theatre at an affordable price to people from all walks of life." **Zadie Smith**

Kiln Theatre sits in the heart of Kilburn in Brent, a unique and culturally diverse area of London where over 140 languages are spoken. We are a welcoming and proudly local venue, with an internationally acclaimed programme of world and UK premieres. Our work presents the world through a variety of lenses, amplifying unheard/ignored voices into the mainstream, exploring and examining the threads of human connection that cross race, culture and identity.

"This place was a special cocoon. Now she has grown and blossomed into a beautiful butterfly." **Sharon D Clarke**

We believe that theatre is for all and want everyone to feel welcome and entitled to call the Kiln their own. We are committed to nurturing the talent of young people and local communities, to provide a platform for their voices to be heard.

"I wanted to say thank you for creating the most diverse theatre I have been to. In terms of race, culture, class, age, everything – not only in the selection of shows and actors, but in the audience." **Audience member**

Kiln Theatre, 269 Kilburn High Road,
London, NW6 7JR
KilnTheatre.com | info@KilnTheatre.com
🖪 ⊚ 𝕏 ▶ ◑ @KilnTheatre

Supported by
ARTS COUNCIL
ENGLAND

Registration No. 1396429.
Registered Charity No. 276892

CREATIVE ENGAGEMENT AT KILN THEATRE

From workshops to performances to events, we create free projects with and for people who live, learn or earn in Brent and North West London. Children, young people and adults from local communities are encouraged to have fun, be inspired, aspire, and have their voices heard through connection, skills building and theatre-making.

SCHOOLS

We ensure our work is affordable and accessible to local schools. Our Schools Programme includes Backstage Workshops, Teachers' Workshops and Networks, Resource Packs and bespoke School Residencies.

YOUTH & PATHWAYS

The Youth & Pathways programme aims to develop the next generation of artists and audiences and create direct and transparent pathways into Kiln and out to the wider theatre ecology. Our 12–15 Youth Theatre and 16–18 Young Company support participants' development through devising and performing in multi-media productions. Kiln Collaborators receive paid training (at London Living Wage) in facilitation, leadership and theatre-making, and support the delivery and development of our Youth strand. We also deliver Fullworks, a week-long programme where young people learn from all departments at Kiln Theatre and attend a Creative Careers fair led by industry professionals, which is open to young people across London

ARRIVE, BUILD, CREATE

Arrive, Build, Create, formerly known as Minding the Gap, has been running for 18 years. We work with local schools and colleges' EAL and ESOL departments to provide creative drama-based sessions for newly arrived young people, which aim to develop creativity, confidence and engagement in the arts. Additionally, we deliver opportunities for participants who wish to develop their skills further, including a Trainee programme, through which former participants receive paid training (at London Living Wage) in facilitation and theatre-making to support the delivery of the programme and a Young Company. We have also produced a Resource Pack and Teacher's CPD for EAL/ESOL teachers across London.

COMMUNITIES

The Communities work is rooted in Kilburn and Brent and celebrates the unique cultural and artistic life of our local area. Activity includes Dementia-friendly Screenings, and Kiln Masterclasses. This year we began delivery on Celebrating Our Stories: the Kilburn High Road Project, made possible with The National Lottery Heritage Fund with thanks to National Lottery Players. This three-year heritage-focused project celebrates and platforms the hidden stories of the High Road and the residents, artists, businesses and organisations who call Kilburn home. Activity in Year One includes a Community Company with newly arrived adults with experience of migration; Chronicles of Kilburn, heritage-inspired workshops in collaboration with local organisations, an oral history expert and artists; Move at the Movies, a movement-based cinema programme working with adults referred through social prescribers; community co-curated Town Hall Talks, a full-day takeover of the building by local artists, organisations and residents; and Listen Local Young Writers, a project which supports 10 local young people aged 18–30 to write their first short plays inspired by their connection to Kilburn and research at Brent Museum and Archives.

For more information about our work and how to get involved, see our website **kilntheatre.com/ creative-engagement**, email us on **getinvolved@kilntheatre.com** or WhatsApp us on **07375 532006**.

SUPPORT OUR WORK

Kiln Theatre is a proudly local theatre with a world-class reputation. We create bold and engaging work which amplifies unheard voices. We are committed to staging extraordinary theatre, inspiring the next generation of artists, and keeping our ticket prices as low as possible.

Every year, we must raise close to **£1 million** to keep our doors open and our lights on. Will you help us?

BECOME A KILN FRIEND

From just **£5 per month**, you can enjoy:

- Access to Priority Booking
- Exclusive updates and insights from Kiln
- Invitations to special Supporters' events

You can also become a Kiln Friend at **Silver** or **Gold** level, which offers an even wider range of exciting opportunities.

Scan the QR code to become a Kiln Friend today!

OTHER WAYS TO GIVE

- Donating when you book tickets
- Naming a Seat
- Remembering us in your will
- Partnering with us through your company
- Introducing us to your Trust or Foundation

KILN CIRCLE

The Kiln Circle is a philanthropic supporters' group that sits at the heart of our theatre. The Circle are given special opportunities to get close to the work on our stage and the artists involved in each of our productions. Donations start from £2,500 per year.

If you wish to join the Kiln Circle or hear more about philanthropy at Kiln, please get in touch with Catherine Walker catherinewalker@kilntheatre.com or 020 7625 0135.

Scan the QR code, visit **Kilntheatre.com/give** or call our Fundraising Team on **020 7625 0132** to join our community of supporters today.

Registered with FUNDRAISING **REGULATOR**

Registered Charity No. 276892

x

THANK YOU

We depend on donations of all sizes to ensure we can fulfil our mission to champion unheard voices and to make theatre for everyone. We would not be able to continue our work without the support of the following:

STATUTORY FUNDERS

Arts Council England
Brent Council Warm Spaces
Camden Council Culture Service
National Lottery Heritage Fund

COMPANIES

The Agency (London) Ltd
Bloomberg Philanthropies
Investec
Nick Hern Books
Vogue World Fund

MAJOR DONORS AND KILN CIRCLE

Nick and Aleksandra Barnes
The Basden Family
Primrose and David Bell
Torrence Boone
Jules and Cheryl Burns
Mary and Jim Callaghan
Laure Zanchi Duvoisin
Dasha Epstein
Gary and Carol Fethke
Matthew Greenburgh and Helen Payne
Ros and Alan Haigh
Mary Clancy Hatch
Linda Keenan
Adam Kenwright
Jonathan Levy and Gabrielle Rifkind
Brian and Clare Linden

Frances Magee
Dame Susie Sainsbury
Jon and NoraLee Sedmak
Dr Miriam Stoppard
Jan and Michael Topham

INDIVIDUALS AND LEGACIES

Sue Fletcher
Nazima Kadir and Karl Gorz
Frances Lynn
Alison McLean and Michael Farthing
In memory of Harry Frank Rose
Ann and Peter Sprinz
Sarah and Joseph Zarfaty

TRUSTS AND FOUNDATIONS

29th May 1961 Charitable Trust
The Atkin Foundation
The Austin and Hope Pilkington Trust
Backstage Trust
Bertha Foundation
Boris Karloff Charitable Foundation
Chapman Charitable Trust
Christina Smith Foundation
City Bridge Foundation – London's biggest independent charity funder
Cockayne Grants for the Arts, a donor advised fund held at the London Community Foundation

John S Cohen Foundation
The D'Oyly Carte Charitable Trust
Esmée Fairbairn Foundation
The Foyle Foundation
Garfield Weston Foundation
Garrick Charitable Trust
The Hobson Charity
Jack Petchey Foundation
John Lyon's Charity
John Thaw Foundation
The Mackintosh Foundation
Marie-Louise von Motesiczky Charitable Trust
The Noël Coward Foundation
Pears Foundation
Richard Radcliffe Trust
The Roddick Foundation
Royal Victoria Hall Foundation
Stanley Thomas Johnson Foundation
Theatre Artists Pilot Programme
Three Monkies Trust
Vanderbilt Family Foundation
The Vandervell Foundation

And all those who wish to remain anonymous.

FOR KILN THEATRE

Pins and Needles

Scene One: Mary

A refrain of a song – 'Hush, Little Baby' – plays and then fades down.

A writer, **Rob Drummond***, leads a middle-aged woman,* **Mary Jones***, into a nondescript room towards a table, surrounded by chairs.* **Mary** *looks around as she sits down.*

Rob   Yeah. It's not the best.

Water?

Mary   Yes please.

You don't have an office?

Rob   The eh . . . the room belongs to the theatre . . .

Mary   The Tricycle . . .

Rob   Yes. They let me use it to, eh . . . do these interviews.

Mary   You do this a lot?

Rob   No. Eh. Well . . . I . . . I'm still relatively early. In my career. I usually just . . . make my plays up but this one is going to be verbatim. I think.

Mary   Verbatim?

Rob   Yeah. I interview you then . . . that becomes the play.

Mary   Word for word?

Rob   I might edit a bit but I won't change the meaning of what you say.

Mary *considers this.*

Mary   So this is going to be on stage?

Rob   Some of it. Yes. Maybe all of it. I don't know yet.

Pause.

Mary   And someone will play me?

Rob   Yes.

Mary   Who?

Rob   I don't know yet.

Mary   Helen Mirren. I know she's not black but I don't care, I love her.

Rob   Well. I'm not sure she'd be . . . Yeah. We can try. Why not?

Can I start recording?

Mary   OK.

Rob   I'll need you to sign this. To allow me to use your words. If that's OK.

Mary *reads.*

Rob   Yes. Please. Take your time.

Mary *reads then signs the document.* **Rob** *waits.*

Rob   Great. So . . .

Mary   So . . .

Rob   Tell me a bit about yourself.

Mary   Eh . . . I'm Mary Jones. I won't tell you my age . . .

She laughs nervously.

I eh . . .

Rob   What do you do for a living?

Mary   I'm a researcher in evolutionary science and I worked for the University of Gloucestershire, but now I, eh, I look after my sons, full time.

Rob   What are your sons called?

Mary   Emmanuel, he's the eldest. And David. His little brother.

Rob   Emmanuel?

Mary   God with us. Good for a girl or a boy. My parents were from Zimbabwe, eh, Rhodesia, as it was called. They came over in the seventies and I was born soon after.

I met my husband here, while studying. Jack. He's a doctor.

We named Emmanuel after my father. David after his.

We worried, you know, that David would have a better chance of success, because his name was more . . . English sounding . . . like we'd accidentally set a little social experiment running . . . but in the end, that was the least of our worries.

Pause.

Sorry. I'm rabbiting.

Rob   It's fine. Say as much or as little as you like.

Mary   You can always edit.

Rob   Yeah. Yeah.

Mary   How did you find me?

Rob   Sorry?

Mary   They called me to ask if I wouldn't mind speaking to you . . . but I don't know how you even . . .

Rob   I read about it. About you. In the paper.

Mary   And you thought . . .

Rob   I thought it was interesting.

Pause. **Mary** *looks at* **Rob**.

Rob   I'm really not going to make any moral or ethical judgement here. I just want the truth.

Mary   Right. Yes.

Rob   Why did you agree? To do this?

Mary   I, eh . . . I just want people to know . . . the whole story.

He was the loveliest, smiliest little boy you know. Emmanuel. I swear he laughed for the first time at three days old. Jack insists it was just gas but . . . He was always just so . . . affectionate.

Until . . .

It was really quite sudden. One morning, when Rutendo was around one year old . . . he stopped making eye contact with us. Stopped smiling. Wasn't as verbal as he had been. And, after a few days of this . . . we kind of guessed – didn't want to believe it but . . . autism seemed likely and we turned out to be correct.

It broke my heart. Like Emmanuel had died and . . . someone else had taken his place. And, of course, we learned to love the new Emmanuel but . . . he was not the same boy.

Pause.

And then we found out it was our fault.

Scene Two: Robert

Robert Hewitt *enters the space.* **Rob** *leaves* **Mary** *and hurries to greet him.*

Rob   Ah.

Robert   Rob?

Rob   Yes. How you doing?

They shake hands.

You found the place OK then?

Robert *looks around.*

Rob   Yeah. It's not the best.

Robert   It's fine.

Rob   The theatre let me use it. To interview people.

Robert   OK.

Silence.

Rob   Do you mind if I start recording?

Robert   Not at all. I'll be recording too.

He takes out his own phone.

Rob   Right. OK. If you like.

Robert   Can't be too careful.

They both start recording. **Mary** *is still in the space but neither man seems to notice her.*

Rob   And you'll need to sign this release form. So I can use what you say in the show.

Robert *takes the form. Glances at it.*

Robert   Who do you work for?

Rob   Eh . . . myself. I'm self-employed.

Robert   Yeah, but . . . on this project. Who's paying you?

Rob   Kiln Theatre.

Robert   I see.

Rob   Is that a problem?

Robert   No. I just always like to know where the money is coming from. I don't think enough people think about that.

Pause.

You read about me online then? About what I did.

Rob   Yes.

Robert   Uh-huh.

And what's your angle?

Rob   Angle?

Robert   Yeah.

Rob   I don't have an angle.

Robert   That's impossible.

Rob   I just want to understand your point of view.

Robert   And then use it for what?

Rob   To write a play.

Robert   And what's the play trying to do?

Rob   Just to get to the truth. About all this.

Pause. **Robert** *scans the document.*

Robert   How many plays you written?

Rob   Oh, eh . . . lots. You don't have to worry. I know what I'm doing.

Silence. **Robert** *keeps reading the document.*

Robert   Can I read the play first? Before I sign off on it.

Rob   You can read it, yes, and I will take into account any concerns, but I'll have the final word.

Robert *sighs.*

Rob   All I can say is that I won't change anything you say. I might edit for clarity and impact but . . .

Robert   Clarity and impact.

Rob   I might change the order of what you say, but not the specific words or . . . meaning. I won't make any moral or ethical judgements at all.

Long pause. **Robert** *considers this.*

Robert   And it'll definitely be on stage?

Rob   If the theatre likes it.

Robert   Sometimes they don't?

Rob   Sometimes. And sometimes it just . . . doesn't happen
. . . for no good reason. The subject matter might . . . go out
of fashion or . . . for example, I interviewed a woman about
a decade ago, about her child who developed autism . . .

Mary *moves in her seat.*

Rob. . . and . . . that play never happened but then . . .
Covid, you know, and suddenly I think, well, I can use that
interview, and yours, because the vaccine topic is . . . back in.
You know?

Robert *nods. Reads the document. Takes his time. Then, finally,
suddenly, signs.*

Robert   So. What do you want to know?

Rob   Start with your name. Age. Occupation. That sort
of thing.

Robert   I'm Robert Hewitt.

Rob   Good name.

Robert   Sorry?

Rob   Robert.

Robert   Oh. Yeah. You can change it if you like. If you think
it will confuse people. The audience. Two Roberts.

Rob   Well, I'm Rob. So it should be fine.

I like it actually. It kind of reinforces that the play is based on
real people. Because I wouldn't choose two such similar
names if I was making it up.

Pause. **Robert** *nods.*

Rob   Please go on.

Robert   Eh . . .

Rob   Age. Occupation . . .

Robert   Right. I'm thirty-five. Unemployed. As of . . . a year ago.

Rob   Yeah.

Robert   Yeah.

Pause.

Rob   What did you do?

Robert   Team leader at a call centre. Dull. Sorry.

Rob   No, no, just trying to get a picture of . . .

Robert   Yeah. I get it.

Pause.

I don't mean to be suspicious. Well, I guess I do. But I wasn't always like this. My mum was religious. She taught me to trust in God and . . . everything would be OK. But that's not true is it?

Rob *says nothing.*

Robert   Mum always said God is infallible. But men are weak and deeply flawed. One day, when I was about eight, I remember asking her how we could trust the Bible, if it was written by men.

She didn't like that.

Pause.

She was right though. Men. People. Are flawed. They do whatever's best for them, right?

Rob   I suppose. Usually.

Robert   And people run institutions, right?

Rob   Yes.

Robert   So institutions do what's best for them. Right?

Rob *concedes.*

Robert   Government, police, big tech, big pharma, legacy media – they all lie to consolidate power. Right?

So why are people so surprised, so outraged, when I dare to suggest one more lie? Every single institution in the world used Covid to maximise profits. It's what they do. When disaster strikes. It's human nature. How can we turn this into a benefit?

For big pharma, Covid was not a disaster. It was the holy grail.

People ask me, why would they lie about vaccines?

The answer is not complicated.

Robert *stares at* **Rob** *and rubs his fingers together.*

Rob   Money.

Robert *nods.* **Rob** *thinks.*

Rob   People might see that as a conspiracy theory.

Robert *laughs.*

Robert   You don't need a conspiracy where interests converge. You don't need secret meetings. It happens naturally. It's evolution. Get power, keep power, survive.

Why would they lie? Ha. Why wouldn't they?

One thing I've learned. From everything that's happened to me . . .

There is no ultimate authority.

Trust no one.

Pause.

Rob   Why did you agree to do this interview, Robert?

Robert   Because I want justice. For my mum.

Silence.

Scene Three: Edward

Edward Jenner, *a man from a different world altogether, enters the space. He is slightly overweight, fifty-three years old with grey hair in a Titus style, and dressed in a smart yellow waistcoat with a cravat, tailcoats and pantaloons with long regency knee socks.*

Edward   Is there no one here to announce me?

Mary *and* **Robert** *are still in the space, but do not notice this man, nor each other. Only* **Rob** *seems to see him.*

Rob   Oh. No. Sorry. We don't really do that anymore.

Please, come in.

Edward *comes in, looking around at the space.*

Rob   I hope this will do.

Edward   I am as comfortable in a hovel as a palace.

Rob   Yes. Right.

Edward   So.

Let me see if I understand this. You have conducted two interviews, one in the year of our lord two thousand and twelve . . .

Rob   With Mary, yes. Back when I was still a bit . . . nervous and . . . didn't really know what I was doing.

Edward   And one in two thousand and twenty-three . . .

Rob   With Robert.

Edward   By which time you had mastered your art.

Rob   I wouldn't say mastered.

Edward   Both interviews on the topic of vaccines.

Rob   Yes.

Edward   And now you wish to interview me. A man over two hundred years dead.

Rob   Yes.

Edward   And you see no problem with this?

Rob   Well. Obviously I can't talk directly to you, but I can read your work. Your diaries. Scientific papers. The transcript of your House of Commons committee hearing. There's a lot there. And I can construct an interview which is, if not fully verbatim, as close an approximation as I can manage. To go along with the other two, genuine verbatim pieces.

Edward   I see. Yes. That is . . . moderately clever.

Perhaps I could help you along the way?

Rob   Help me?

Edward   Construct the play. I am something of an artist myself you know. I write poetry.

Rob   Yes I know, I read Signs of Rain.

Edward   Oh it has survived then, how flattering. What did you think?

Rob   I . . . eh . . . it rhymed.

Edward
   The hollow winds begin to blow,
   The clouds look back, the grass is low,
   The soot falls down, the spaniels sleep,
   And spiders from their cobwebs peep.

Rob *nods politely.*

Edward   Thank you, thank you. Of course, poetry is not the end of my artistic endeavours. I play piano. And violin.

Rob   Yes.

Edward   Perhaps the actor who will be playing me should be a musician too.

Rob   Perhaps.

Edward   Then you could bring music to the piece.

Rob   That's a nice idea.

Edward   So where do I sign?

Rob   You don't really need to . . . I mean, you're dead so you can't sue us if we . . .

Edward *is staring at* **Rob**.

Rob   Sign here.

Edward *signs*.

Edward   Doctor. Edward. Jenner. There.

I am also a naturalist you know.

Rob   Yes.

Edward   I discovered birds fly south for the winter rather than burrowing underground.

Rob   People used to think . . . birds . . . burrowed?

Edward   And it was I who first realised what was going on with cuckoos.

Rob   You mean when they lay their eggs in other . . .

Edward   I spent hours, days, watching this one nest. The cuckoo egg hatched and I watched with amazement as this new-born creature managed to hoist the other eggs out of the nest.

I cut it open in the end. Dissected it. And found that God had given him a little nook in the back of his neck, perfectly designed to carry eggs. Remarkable.

Rob   Right. So you're a man of many talents.

Edward   Napoleon is a fan.

Rob   I'm sorry, what?

Edward   Napoleon. He is a fan of mine. I shared some of my research with him. Probably saved the lives of thousands of his soldiers, countrymen, children. Of course people accused me of aiding in their war effort – of being a traitor – but I don't see it like that. I see children dying and . . . I mean, what other option did I have?

Rob   Well, that's what I want to talk to you about. Your research. Your vaccine.

Edward   Why? Does it no longer work?

Rob   No, no. It works. It worked. I mean . . . smallpox no longer exists but . . .

Edward   It no longer exists? What? In Britain?

Rob   In the world.

Stunned silence. **Edward** *sits down.*

Edward   I must be the most famous man who ever lived.

Pause.

Rob   Well . . . I mean, I did have to google.

Edward   Google?

Rob   To find you.

Edward *looks blankly at* **Rob**.

Edward   Smallpox eradicated.

Rob *nods.*

Edward   So I am vindicated.

Ha.

Just two hundred years too late.

Rob   Too late for what?

Edward   To clear my name.

Rob   Ah yes. Of course. All that stuff with the House of Commons committee and . . . the anti-vaxxers.

Edward   Anti-vaxxers?

Rob   It's what we call people who are opposed to vaccinations.

Edward   I thought you said that smallpox was gone.

Rob   Yes but . . . I mean, your technology has become . . . we have vaccines for all sorts of diseases.

Edward   And people still oppose them?

Rob   Well . . . they have their reasons.

Edward *approaches* **Mary** *and* **Robert**, *still both oblivious.*

Edward   Are these two . . . anti-vaxxers?

Rob   No, no. You can't see them. Or hear them.

Edward   I most certainly can.

Rob   Well, no. For this to work, you three need to be separate. Three different interviews. Across time. OK?

Edward   Wouldn't it be better if we all just . . . chatted?

Rob   It wouldn't be verbatim.

Pause. **Edward** *suddenly pulls a violin from nowhere.*

Edward   Would you like me to play? Throughout the piece. As a kind of . . . motif.

Pause.

Rob   If you like.

Edward *plays the violin. 'Hush, Little Baby'.*

(*This may return throughout, as desired.*)

Scene Four: The Question

Mary, **Robert**, *and* **Edward**, *still in the same space, but not aware of each other.*

Mary   So. Where do I begin?

Robert   Where do you want me to start?

Rob   Wherever you like. I'm just here to . . . facilitate.

Edward   Perhaps the scientific method might be a good . . . framing device. For the piece.

Rob   Well, actually, you don't know about the scientific method. It was codified in the 1930s. I mean, you do know about it, you use it, essentially, but you don't call it that, yet, so you can't . . .

But you might be onto something.

Edward   I usually am.

Rob   Because Mary talked about the scientific method in her interview I seem to remember. Let me just . . .

Yes. Here.

Mary   There are five stages to the scientific method – well, more in some models but I was always taught five.

Stage one is to define a question. Something you want to investigate.

Rob   Yes. That's what playwrights say too. When you're writing a play. You need a question to . . . concentrate on. To keep it . . . neat, tidy . . .

Mary   Same with a PhD.

Mine was called . . .

'From Instinctual Responses to Complex Social Strategies: An Evolutionary Analysis of the Development of Trust and Doubt Mechanisms in Protohuman Societies and Their Role in the Formation of Cooperative Behaviours and Intergroup Dynamics.'

Rob   Catchy title.

Mary   Thank you. My question was basically . . . how did we evolve trust and doubt at the same time?

Rob   Trust and doubt.

Mary   Yes. We didn't evolve, initially, to . . . know ourselves . . . to be ultra-self-aware . . . so the doubt part . . . that came first. That is older. Every single noise is a danger. Question everything. Doubt everything. Run!

The only thing we trusted, instinctively, was our parents. The first, and ultimate, authority figures in our lives.

And then . . . eh . . . the pre-frontal cortex, that's the bit at the front of the brain which basically controls emotions and thoughts, that got bigger and bigger over time because, well . . . it helped us to differentiate between real and imagined dangers and become more sophisticated, but the underlying fear . . . the baseline of . . . better safe than sorry . . . that remained. And has remained ever since.

So, you see, we can't help but doubt. It is what got us here. It is us.

Rob *nods.*

Rob   You mentioned parents. What were yours like?

Mary   My parents? They were . . .

They trusted their own instincts. Above anything else. Learned that from their parents. From their extended family. From bitter experience of being screwed by authority at every turn. Back home. And then again when they came here. When I said I wanted to be a scientist my mum told me to watch out. I might care about science but science doesn't care about people like me.

I do carry some of that with me. I must do. But . . .

Science gave me a way out. A way of . . . looking at the world less emotionally. Of trying to work out what the truth was. Regardless of the . . .. politics. You know?

Sorry. What was the question?

Pause.

Robert The question is, how have they got away with it?

Rob With what?

Robert With killing so many people.

Rob Well . . . that's a big claim.

Robert Is your mum still living, Rob?

Rob I don't really want to insert myself into the play.

Robert You don't have to. Just answer the question.

Pause.

Rob No. She's not.

Robert Right. I'm sorry to hear that. Did you get on with her? When she was alive?

Rob Yes.

Silence. **Rob**'s *not giving any more.*

Robert My mum . . .

Me and my mum were . . .

Dad left when I was six so she brought me up on her own.

She looked after me till I was old enough to look after her.

We were a team. You know.

I've got a mum tattoo you know. Right here.

He shows a tattoo on his arm.

I loved her so much.

Pause.

I was already wary, man, but . . . see when they locked us all down. I had the time to properly research it all. For the first time. Online and that and . . .

They knew, you know. They knew lockdown would cause excess suicides, alcoholism, missed cancer diagnosis, loss of livelihood. But they didn't care. Because there was power to be consolidated and money to be made.

They locked us down while they were having parties and groping their secretaries' arses in cupboards. And gave almost two billion pounds of our money to their mates' companies.

Keep them scared. Frighten the pants off them with the new strain. And *that's* verbatim. Text messages from that Hancock prick.

Do you think it's any different with the vaccines? Pfizer made billions. You expect me to believe they didn't know, in advance, that their product caused blood clots? That people were absolutely going to die?

Rob   So are you . . . I mean . . . do you believe the vaccines work or . . .

Robert   I believe that we have been lied to at every conceivable level. So only a moron would think that the vaccines were not part of that.

Rob   But . . . I mean, every vaccine ever released is dangerous to a very small percentage of the population. Are you saying this vaccine is worse?

Robert   I'm not a scientist. Neither are you. What you need to ask yourself is why are you so certain they do work? You just trust what you're told. By people who have a proven track record of lying for profit. Why do you believe they do work? Eh?

Rob   I don't want to get too involved in . . .

Robert   Do you deny that the Pfizer vaccine has been shown to cause myocarditis?

Rob   Covid also causes myocarditis. Usually worse . . .

Robert   My mum, who was perfectly healthy before she got her jab, died from myocarditis. She was killed by her Pfizer vaccine. Killed by the thing they told her was to protect her from dying.

How would you feel if that was your mum?

Pause. **Rob** *thinks.*

Robert   And it wasn't just her. There's a hundred stories. A thousand. Are you going to ignore them all?

Edward   Stories? Stories?!

Rob   No. Remember, you can't hear him.

Edward *shouts directly at* **Robert**.

Edward   The plural of anecdote, young man, is not evidence.

Rob   He can't hear you.

Edward   Well, I wish he could.

We must not believe anecdotal things without testing. Any number of factors could render the anecdote wrong. Personal error, lies, preferential bias . . .

Rob   Feelings.

Edward   We must not let our feelings get in the way of the truth. That is not to say we ignore them. Only that we understand they can sometimes affect our reasoning. Humans are so fallible when using their gut – the scientific method, as you call it, is a better system.

Rob   But any system can be corrupted.

Robert   All humans are corrupt. All systems are run by humans. Therefore all systems are corrupt.

Mary   The real problem is, most of us don't have the time to become an expert in any given important issue, so we simply *have* to trust the experts. The data they produce. The papers they write.

So the question is . . . the question has to be . . . how do you know what, and who to trust? How do you know what to believe?

Rob   So what's the answer?

Mary *smiles.*

Scene Five: Predictions

Mary *takes centre stage.*

Mary   In stage two of the scientific method you make a prediction. A testable statement that you think will describe the outcome of an investigation into your question.

Rob   So, if my question, in this play I'm trying to write about you is . . . how do you know who to trust . . . then . . . what's our prediction?

Mary   Well, just come up with something. The beauty of the scientific method is being wrong is fine.

Rob   OK. Well. I would predict that . . . you shouldn't trust someone or any organisation that stands to make financial or political benefit from a claim.

Mary   Is it not possible to make money *and* tell the truth? Big pharma may well be corrupt, but they only make a profit when the medicine actually works.

Rob   Right. Yes. So I need to alter my prediction already.

Mary   How about . . . *be more wary* of anyone who stands to gain from a claim.

Pause.

Rob   Tell us about Andrew Wakefield's paper.

Pause.

Mary   Well. His question was . . . what is causing autism in children?

A fine question to ask.

His prediction was that it was caused by a vaccine-induced bowel disorder in early childhood.

And, to my shock, his paper, peer reviewed and published in *The Lancet*, a British Medical Journal established in 1823 . . .

Edward   My Lord, Mary, that's the year I died.

Rob   Quiet.

Mary   Proved his prediction to be true.

The newspapers all covered it.

This would have been, eh . . . 1998.

New study confirms link between MMR vaccine and autism. Front-page story.

I looked up the paper. And sure enough, twelve respected research scientists had put their name to it.

Twelve. So I didn't have to trust one man. And none of them had anything to gain from lying, not that I could tell.

This was a peer-reviewed study. Which demonstrated a link between the MMR vaccine, which Emmanuel had been given . . . and autism, with which he had subsequently been diagnosed.

We didn't want to admit it, me and Jack, but it made absolute sense.

It was science . . . science to confirm all the suspicions I grew up around. Science to say that science was wrong! That we shouldn't trust those who claimed to know what was best for us.

My mum could barely conceal her delight. See! See! I told you you can't trust them. Putting chemicals into your body! See!

But all we could think was . . . my God. We caused Emmanuel's autism.

Silence.

Do you have children?

Rob   This is meant to be about you.

Mary   Do you have kids?

Pause.

Rob   Not yet.

Mary *smiles.*

Mary   Working on it?

Rob   We're . . . I'm not sure I want them.

Mary   Why not?

Pause.

Rob   I . . . there's a couple of reasons, but . . .

Mainly I just . . .

The state of the world, you know. Is it ethical to bring another . . .

Sorry. Look. I don't want to insert myself into the play.

Edward   Bit late for that isn't it?

Rob   I don't want it to get messy.

Edward   Yes. Let's get messy! Art is messy. Science is neat. They both seek truth, but only one is permitted to lie to get there.

Am I right, Rob?

He winks.

Rob Look, this section is about predictions. We have to keep focussed on predictions.

Robert The prediction was that Mum would get the vaccine and be protected from Covid.

Edward The prediction was? Did he really word it like that? Seems a bit convenient. For the predictions section of the play.

Rob Yes. Right. I've changed it a bit. It's still verbatim. More or less.

Edward More or less.

Robert I trusted the guidelines.

I didn't see my mum for months. Just put food on her doorstep and waved from the bottom of the garden. Like a chump.

I started drinking more. In the house. Like half the fucking country. Spending more time online. A lot more time.

And then the vaccines came. Mum wasn't in the vulnerable category so she had to wait. She was scared. She didn't want it. The vaccine. But I . . . I convinced her.

I actually convinced her to take it.

I was still naive back then.

Ha.

And one week later . . .

She died.

Pause.

I didn't think anything of it, at first. I mean, she was in her sixties. Heart attacks happen but . . . then, a month after that, I read about it online. About Pfizer. And . . .

She was already buried.

Pause.

Rob   So you were trying to answer the question . . . what killed my mum? And your prediction was that it was the Pfizer vaccine.

Robert   She was in perfect health. She was given the vaccine. She died of a heart attack. What else could it have been?

Pause.

Mary   Emmanuel was a normal little boy. We gave him his MMR. And suddenly . . . he couldn't smile. Make eye contact. What else could it have been?

Edward   Correlation is not causation.

Rob   Not always. But it can be.

Edward   Yes, and it's the scientist's job to discern when a prediction is true and when it is simply a coincidence.

Rob   How?

Edward   Well, that is stage three so I'm assuming you don't want to get into that now. To keep things . . . neat.

Pause.

Rob   What question were you trying to answer? In your work?

Edward   That's simple. How do we stop people, children dying of smallpox?

Rob   And what was your prediction?

Edward   That if I infected them with cowpox, they would be immune to smallpox.

Rob   Why did you think that?

Edward   Simple. I noticed milkmaids didn't seem to catch smallpox.

Rob   Huh.

Edward   The only treatment for smallpox at the time was . . . barbaric.

Variolation they called it. It was done to me. As a schoolboy.

I was bled, repeatedly, . . . bled until I was feeble and emaciated, to purify my blood. Purify my blood. A phrase without meaning. A practice without reason.

I was taken, with a load of other boys . . . to a large room. An inoculation station.

We were jabbed with needles – needles which had been previously exposed to live smallpox pustules.

Rob   So to prevent smallpox, you infected children with . . . smallpox.

Edward   Essentially. Yes.

The prediction was that we might suffer a mild, controlled bout of smallpox, which would make us immune in the future.

And they were right. About the immunity part. But there is no such thing as a mild form of smallpox.

Let me tell you.

There is no disease that the medical writer has to describe which presents a melancholier scene than the natural smallpox as it very frequently occurs.

The symptoms bring on pain and debilitation. A terrible feeling of anxiety. High temperature, unquenchable thirst, diarrhoea, inflammation of the eyes.

Violent sweating. Convulsions.

Many speck like spots that become red and painful and turn to pustules.

By the seventh day the eyelids will often swell and stick together causing loss of vision.

Fitful and disturbed sleep. Each morning would bring a horrid scene of gore mingled with corruption.

Death would relieve the sufferer between the fourteenth and seventeenth day.

Those who survived would often be blind and scarred for life. Physically and mentally.

Thirty-five per cent of child deaths are caused by smallpox.

. . .

I was eight and I remember wishing for death. To take away the pain.

I survived. Gained immunity to the virus, as intended. Some of my classmates were not so lucky.

For years afterwards I carried with me a certain . . . traumatic shadow of the event. Like I was both immune to smallpox but nonetheless carried it with me every day. It is probably, in hindsight, the reason I vowed to find a more humane way.

And I did. But I needed to gather data to prove it.

Scene Six: Data

Mary   Stage three is gathering data. Collecting the material you will need to either prove or disprove your prediction.

Rob   So if our prediction is that you should be wary of anyone who has something to gain from a claim then . . .

Mary   You need data to demonstrate the accuracy of that prediction.

Rob   Like what?

Mary   Like an experiment where you gather a group of people and tell them not to lie. Then pay some of them to break the rules. And see if they do.

Rob   Seems obvious they would.

Mary   But then you raise the stakes. So their lies might harm others. That's the real test. Will our evolved sense of selfishness overcome our evolved sense of morality? Or vice versa.

Rob   And which is it?

Mary   Well . . . it's not that straightforward.

Pause.

In Zimbabwe, my mother told me, the government accepted bribes to allow big pharmaceutical companies to conduct clinical trials on the people. They told the people the trials were totally safe. They lied. For money. My mother's sister took part in one of the trials. She was made infertile.

It's easy to see why Mum never trusted authority.

But . . . the trials, which made some women infertile, helped the drug company come up with a genuinely safe product. In the end. And that drug was then given to the Zimbabwean government in return for keeping schtum about the trials.

And that drug saved lives. Many thousands more than it ruined.

So . . .

None of this is simple, you see.

Robert   It's simple. My mum was killed by the vaccine. And she wasn't alone. I found others. Online. Who had lost relatives shortly after receiving the jab.

I went to protest marches. There was a big one. In London. You probably saw footage. And . . .

My face was all over social media so my boss found out and . . .

He fired me.

For being on a march.

Fired me for having an opinion.

That's not right, right?

Rob   I agree. That's . . .

I agree.

Pause.

Robert   Some of the people I met on the marches had applied to this government scheme. The Vaccine Damage Payment Scheme. A hundred and twenty grand if an autopsy proves your loved one died as a direct result of a Covid vaccine.

I couldn't have cared less about the money. I just wanted them to admit what they had done.

To my mum.

But I needed data.

Edward *laughs.*

Rob   Yes, OK. He said evidence but . . .

Edward   This is the data section of the play. Don't worry. It's fine. Small lie. Bigger truth.

Rob   Exactly.

Robert   I needed data.

But the data was in the ground.

In my mum's body.

What was I meant to do?

Silence.

Mary   I fell pregnant again. Shortly after the Wakefield paper was published.

And we both knew, me and Jack, we had a huge decision to make.

Jack said he would rather have another autistic child than a dead one. Simple as that.

Rob   Right.

Mary   But Jack was wrong. You know. At least, not totally right. He had created a false dichotomy.

He hadn't properly considered the data.

In his head it was either an autistic child or a dead one. But what about a healthy child, with no autism? That was also an option. Not every unvaccinated child dies. In fact, they rarely do. They might have a rough time, if they catch measles or whatever . . . but they usually get through it. That's just a fact.

I went online and looked it up on Yahoo. I gathered the data to support my prediction that it was more of a risk to have our second child vaccinated than not.

I looked up death rates from measles, mumps and rubella.

In 1998 there were 377 cases of measles, almost 4000 cases of mumps and only twelve cases of rubella in England and Wales.

And in of all those cases . . . one died. Just one . . . child.

Rob   It's still a risk.

Mary   That's what being a parent is about. Weighing risks. Let them go out and play and maybe they'll get run over or lost or abducted. But probably not. Keep them locked down . . . in the house . . . and they'll almost definitely become scared and anxious.

Robert *shifts in his chair.*

Rob   But safe.

Mary   Well. There's never actually never been a safer time to be alive in the history of humanity than now.

Rob   Never been a safer time to be . . .

Mary   Statistically. In every measurable way. We've never had it better. The world has never been safer.

Rob   Doesn't feel like that.

Mary   Twenty-four-hour news.

Pause.

Anyway, Jack wouldn't budge. He was certain. He accepted that the paper in *The Lancet* showed a link between the MMR and autism. But he was adamant it was the lesser of two risks.

I love Emmanuel with all my heart. But it breaks me to think of the life he could have had. A fuller life. With a wife and children in his future. Which is possible, I suppose. But extremely unlikely.

If I could protect my second child from that – ensure they had the future he could not – then surely that was the only thing to do.

That's all any of this is about really. Protecting people. Children. Doing what's best for them.

I gave birth to a healthy little boy. We named him David. Emmanuel didn't smile. Didn't bond with him at all. Which only made my convictions stronger.

When David was one year old, it was time to have him vaccinated. With the MMR jab. And Jack was still adamant that we were going to do it. So I caved. I told him I would take him. And Jack seemed so relieved. Told me I was doing the right thing.

So I took David to the hospital for his appointment.

I took him to the hospital. But I didn't take him in.

I decided, as a parent, that it was worth the risk.

Pause.

Edward I knew, going into my clinical trials, that there was a risk. Of course I did. But the benefits would be immeasurable in comparison.

I had to gather the data to prove my prediction. Cowpox would protect against smallpox.

I found a milkmaid, Sarah Nelms, who had fresh cowpox pustules and lesions on her hands and arms, and, using matter from Sarah's lesions, I inoculated a young boy, James Phipps, with cowpox.

Rob You gave him cowpox.

Edward Yes. That is, technically, what inoculation against smallpox is.

Rob But you gave a young child . . . a disease.

Edward We must actually do things, not just talk and think. And in this case, there was no other way of gathering data.

The path of life is full of thorns and if you keep children on velvet until the day comes that they must feel those thorns . . .

Rob And was he ok?

Edward My results are well documented. James Phipps was fine. A slight fever for a few days. Some pustules on the hands and arms. Never any danger to his life. And so, in July of the same year . . . leaving plenty of time for the boy to recover, I inoculated him again. This time with smallpox material taken from the fresh lesion of a smallpox patient.

Rob You gave an eight-year-old boy smallpox.

Edward   No. I did not give him smallpox. I tried to give him smallpox. And singularly failed. Because my inoculation had worked! You see? The cowpox infection protected young James from the smallpox.

I was overjoyed. But I knew this was not conclusive proof.

To convince the world, I had to carry out this process many dozens of times. Document each and every case. Show that inoculation with cowpox, or vaccination, as I called it – from the Latin 'vaccine' for cow – was a reliable and predictable preventer of infection with smallpox.

And that's exactly what I did. And you can see the results. Here. Documented in this publication. *An Inquiry into the Causes and Effects of the Variolae Vaccinae – A Disease Discovered in Some of the Western Counties of England, Particularly Gloucestershire, and Known by the Name of the Cow Pox.*

Rob   Catchy title.

Edward   You've read it?

Rob   Cover to cover.

Edward   And were you convinced?

Rob   Eh. Yes. I have to say I was.

Edward   Dozens of successful cases.

Rob   And one failure.

Silence.

Edward   Yes. one failure.

Rob   Samuel Bradthorne.

Edward   Samuel Bradthorne.

He bows his head.

Robert   Do you know how to get a body exhumed Rob?

Rob   No.

Robert   Nah. We don't know the rules do we? When this sort of thing happens. No one does.

I had no idea what to do. So I did what anyone would.

I googled it.

Ha.

And Google told me that I could apply to the Ministry of Justice. To have her exhumed and autopsied. To prove it was the jab that killed her.

To get the data and apply for the scheme.

So I went online and I downloaded the form. The application form. To get Mum dug up.

And it was . . . well, they don't make it easy.

I needed a funeral director to agree to assist me, and a pathologist to do the autopsy. You see? You see how the system is designed to stop you questioning authority at every stage. Most people would have quit there and then. But I'm not most people.

I went on Twitter.

I found a pathologist. One who reckoned the vaccines were bad.

This pathologist agreed to do the autopsy if we were successful. And he knew a funeral director who would be willing to oversee the exhumation. So . . . suddenly it didn't seem so far fetched.

Maybe I could get justice. For Mum.

I filled in the application. Sent it away. I was confident. It was good. Reasonable. It had the backing of two professionals, you know, proper people. It was going to succeed.

And then the reality of what I was doing hit me. I was going to dig up my mum's body. And have it cut open.

I had nightmares you know. Waiting for the decision. My mum's body coming to visit me in the night. Proper night terrors.

Anyway, the reply finally arrives in the mail and . . . I can't believe it.

Dear Mr Hewitt, we regret to inform you . . .

I mean, just get your head round that, if you can. She's my mother. I paid for her funeral. Her burial. And now, the powers that be tell me they won't allow me to get justice for her.

She's my mum.

My fucking mum.

Pause. He composes himself.

You know they created it in a lab? Covid. Yeah?

Rob   I heard that's looking likely.

Robert   We were called loonies for believing that.

And now we're called loonies for noticing these vaccines are dangerous.

Rob   But are they? Really?

Robert   The European Medicines Agency reported 11,448 people died after taking Covid vaccines. 8368 of them were Pfizer.

Rob   Died after taking the vaccines or because of them?

Robert   Same difference.

Rob   Is it?

Robert   Even the government have admitted they fucked up. They set up that scheme. The vaccine damage payment scheme.

Rob   That was set up in 1979! It covers all vaccines. No one is saying vaccines can never do harm.

5.5 billion people worldwide have had this jab. Of course there will be adverse side effects in some of them.

Robert   Adverse side effects. Say what you mean. Deaths.

Rob   Yes. Deaths. OK. How many more would have died without the jabs though?

Robert   The survival rate from Covid is 99 per cent.

Rob   What's one per cent of eight billion, genius?

Pointing at **Robert**'s *tattoo.*

Rob   Fuckin' tattoos are more likely to kill you than the jabs.

Robert   They were rushed.

Rob   They were rushed because we needed them to be. Every single scientist in the world was working on the problem at the same time! Of course we created them quickly. We had to! It wasn't the dark arts, it was a triumph of human ingenuity and camaraderie.

Robert   They skipped steps.

Rob   What steps? What steps were skipped?

You don't know do you?

You read that online and believed it.

Robert *stares* **Rob** *down.*

Robert   I thought you said you weren't going to judge, Rob? Insert yourself into the play.

Silence.

Rob   I think we need a break.

Robert   Yeah. Good idea.

Mary   I have a headache, Rob, could we . . .

Rob *nods.*

Rob   Ten minutes. Yeah?

Robert *and* **Mary** *nod.* **Rob** *leaves the room.*

Edward, **Mary** *and* **Robert** *sit alone for the first time.*

A long silence.

Edward *stands up. Surveys the scene. Makes sure* **Rob** *has really gone.*

He takes out his violin and plays.

Slowly, **Mary** *and* **Robert** *notice the music, and then* **Edward**. *They look at him.*

Robert   My mum used to sing that to me. When I was wee.

Mary   'Hush Little Baby'. I still sing it. To my kids.

Edward   I played it for my son. In his final days.

Mary   You lost your son?

Edward   Tuberculosis.

Pause.

I'm Edward.

Mary   Mary.

Robert   Robert.

Edward   Would you like some water, Mary?

Mary *nods.*

Robert   Here.

He holds out a bottle. **Edward** *takes it from him and gives it to* **Mary**.

Robert   Paracetamol?

Edward   What's that?

Robert   Pills. For headaches.

He hands them to **Edward**, *who takes them to* **Mary**.

Edward   How do they work?

Robert   They eh . . . I don't know. They just do.

Mary   They block the production of prostaglandins in the brain.

Robert   Yeah. That.

Edward   Prost . . .

Mary   Pain receptors.

Edward   And you use these a lot? Without knowing how they work?

Robert   I don't care how they work. I just know they do. No one ever died from a couple of paracetamol.

Mary   Not true actually. You can die if you're allergic. But it's very rare.

Pause.

Robert   Do you know Rob? The writer?

Edward   I'm helping him. To write his play. I am something of an artist myself you know.

Mary   He's a nice boy.

Robert   Is he?

Mary   Means well. I think.

Pause.

Edward   We're not meant to be talking. Like this.

Mary   Why not?

Edward   Well, it's meant to be verb . . . eh . . .

Robert   Verbatim.

Edward   That's it.

But, between you and me, half the stuff I've said already he just made up.

Robert   Really?

Edward   I didn't even keep a diary.

Robert   So he's lying.

Edward   I don't know if I would call it that.

Robert   How do we know he won't lie about what we say?

Mary   Make us look stupid.

Robert   Crazy.

Edward   I really don't think that's what he wants to do.

But . . . only God can tell our true intentions.

Robert   God?

Wait. Are you . . . Edward Jenner?

Edward   The same.

Robert   Yeah. Rob mentioned you. He's the dude that cured smallpox.

Mary   Oh. Wow. What an honour.

Robert   God died around 1900, mate.

Edward   He . . . died?

Robert   Well. Never existed.

Edward   So who created us?

Mary   No one. We evolved.

Edward   What on earth are you talking about?

Robert   We all came from bacteria, Edward, not dust, not some bloke's rib, not the imagination of a cosmic sky daddy.

Mary   We came from viruses actually. If you want to be specific.

Edward   We came from viruses?

Mary   They were probably the precursors of the first cells. And they've helped shape the genomes of every single species across time. Including humans.

Edward   We came from viruses.

He is staring into space.

Robert   I think you broke Edward.

Mary   I'm sorry, Edward. Do you not believe me?

Edward   No. No. Quite the contrary. It makes complete sense. We come from viruses.

It is quite the most incredible, and yet the most credible thing I have ever heard.

Pause.

Rob *comes back in. Catches them all talking. They scatter. Go back to their own time zones.*

Rob   Were you just . . .

Edward   I just thought it might be useful if . . .

Rob   I've told you. They can't talk to each other. This is real. It's serious.

Edward   They're worried you'll make them look bad.

Rob   I'm not here to judge.

Edward   Yes you are. You think anyone who doesn't believe in vaccinations is a crank and a lunatic of the utmost degree.

Rob   I don't.

Edward Oh, wel,l if you say so. We just have to trust the author. The authority.

Rob You are the authority. On vaccines. Should I not trust you?

Edward Of course you shouldn't! You should look at my research. Replicate my studies if need be. Blind trust is every bit as bad as blind denial.

Rob Oh my God this is impossible. How the hell am I meant to write about all this shit?! Keep everyone happy. Keep my own opinions out of it. Question authority while being the authority. Write the truth while, obviously, having to tell lies here and there because it's a fucking play!

Pause. Everyone is looking at him now.

Edward You should have just written it as a biography. Of me.

Rob Just. Be quiet. Yeah?

Edward If you want me to be quiet, simply stop typing my lines.

Pause. **Rob** *looks directly at* **Edward**.

Rob What is your objective here exactly?

Edward Objective?

Rob Mary wants to explain herself. Robert wants justice.

Edward Oh. Well. I want to save the world.

Rob No. You just seem to be here to . . . aggravate things.

Edward Help.

Rob Help what?

Edward Help you to reach your objective.

Rob How will you aggravating me help me get to the truth?

Edward   The truth? That's not your objective, Rob, come on now.

Rob   It is.

Edward   No, no, no. You just want to convince the audience you're right.

But what happens if you succeed? If one of them gets vaccinated, because of your play. Then dies. Are you ready for that responsibility?

Rob *thinks.*

Rob   Samuel Bradthorne.

Edward *nods.*

Rob   Tell me about him.

Pause. **Rob** *stares at* **Edward**.

Edward   His parents consented. Like all the others. No money changed hands. I did not pay anyone to take part in my trials. They wanted it.

He suffered a very bad reaction to the first vaccine.

Cowpox has been known to kill before. But very rarely. And on this occasion . . . the boy must have had an . . . underlying condition that rendered him . . .

I lost a son you know. I am not heartless. I know the pain Samuel's parents must have felt. But it's not like I killed him. Not really. Not deliberately.

He is the only subject I have lost thus far in my trials. But . . . I am prepared to lose more. In order to save lives. I am sorry if that sounds cold.

You can't have it both ways. You can't accept modern medicine when it suits you and dismiss it when it does not. You either trust science or you don't.

What happened to Samuel was . . . a statistical likelihood.

He stares out into the audience. Silence.

Scene Seven: Analysis

Mary   Stage four. Analyse the data.

Edward   Using tables, graphs or diagrams, scientists look for patterns that show connections between important variables which may be used to prove the prediction correct.

And all my data showed me to be correct about the prophylactic properties of cowpox as relates to smallpox.

Rob   Prophylactic properties?

Edward   Preventative. Cowpox prevents smallpox.

Pause.

Mary   David was healthy. And happy. He looked me in the eyes. Smiled. Just like Emmanuel before we . . .

That was all the analysis of the data I needed. To know my decision not to have him vaccinated was correct.

I knew, in the future, he might have a few days or weeks of discomfort – if and when he caught measles or . . .

But he looked at me. And smiled. And spoke. And laughed. And . . .

And you know the real miracle? David was even bringing Emmanuel out of his shell. Emmanuel isn't stupid you know. He's very smart. He knows what it is to be a big brother. And when David was six, he actually started acting like one.

Asking David if he was being bullied at school. Tucking him into bed at night. Reading him stories. He tried to be a big brother. And he kind of managed it. To an extent. And David loved him. Absolutely adored him. And all the while Jack's there saying, see, it was worth the risk and I'm thinking, ha, what risk? I saved him, not you.

My decision was correct.

The analysis of the data showed it.

Or so I thought.

Edward   In 1797 I presented the analysis of my data to the Royal Society. And what do you think happened?

They rejected it. Told me that my ideas, while not without substance, might be too revolutionary for the time. And that I needed to gather more proof.

More proof?

The analysis was sound.

But, of course, they brought up the boy. Samuel Bradthorne. Said my method was too dangerous. This from the people still propagating the vicious method of variolation.

From which many of them made a lot of money, I may add.

They were not so concerned about the safety of the public as they were with the safety of their income.

Corrupt, the lot of them.

The scientific method is incorruptible, but human beings are certainly not.

Rob   Yes. That's the problem, isn't it? The method is sound but people are not. So how can you blame anyone for having doubts? About anything.

He looks at **Robert**.

Robert   I miss her. My mum.

Rob   Yeah. Me too.

Mine, not yours.

Robert *chuckles*.

Robert   How did she die?

Rob   Do you mind if we stick with your story. For now.

What you did.

Pause. **Robert** *sighs*.

Robert   What I did.

What. I. Did.

It was logical. That's the truth. Despite how the media portrayed me. It was completely logical.

I didn't have any data to analyse. I couldn't prove what I knew to be true. Without digging her up. They wouldn't authorise it. So I had to do it myself.

Pause.

Mary   It was January of last year. 12 January 2011.

David caught the measles.

Jack didn't believe it. He kept saying to the doctor that it was impossible. He's had his MMR.

And the doctor told him, no. He hadn't.

Do you think I'm a fool, Rob?

Pause.

Rob   I, eh . . . I think it's rarely useful to call someone that.

Mary   But you think I am?

Rob   I think it's unfair to judge. I know more than you did at the time you made your decision.

Mary   Yes. Well. Jack wasn't quite so understanding in his analysis.

Pause.

Robert   If I could have her exhumed, in secret, have the autopsy done, properly documented – analyse the data – you know, film all of it – then publish the findings . . .

The pathologist I found online was willing. He was as angry as I was about the whole thing. And he said he would help me find someone to do the exhumation. Someone he knew who was also sympathetic.

We just had to get her out of the ground without anyone knowing and then, afterwards, take our lumps. A fine, jail time, whatever it took. I said I would take the blame. They could just say they were hired by me and were unaware I didn't have permission.

We did it at night. Exhumation is always done at night. So you don't get rubberneckers.

The graveyard where Mum is buried is vast. And it's not locked at night. So . . . we just drove straight in.

The pathologist's friend – he had a van, and in the back was this tiny little excavator. A micro-digger. Ha. The whole thing felt . . . surreal.

He dug down to her in no time. And then we were face to face with the coffin. And it hit me. Mum is in there. My mum.

Who made me breakfast. Who walked me to school. Who put plasters on my knee. Gave me medicine and sang to me.

There but not there. Her but not her. You know?

We had to get the coffin up and out and loaded onto the back of the van but . . . we never got that far.

Someone had seen us. I suppose. Called the police.

We never got her out. Never did the autopsy. Never really got close.

He laughs sadly.

We were all arrested. But I was true to my word. I took the blame. And I don't regret trying. For Mum. I mean, I had to try, right?

Pause.

Mary   Some kids brush measles off, but others, they react really quite badly . . . and David. . . he was just very, very unlucky.

We knew straight away that it was bad.

He quickly got a bacterial ear infection. Which caused him severe pain.

Inflammation of the eyes. Eh, conjunctivitis. They call that.

And then inflammation of the airways. It was one thing after another.

He was sweating and shaking. The doctors did their best to make him comfortable.

And the spots. He couldn't stop scratching them. When he was conscious.

They stabilised him but after a week he lost his vision.

He wasn't getting better so they induced a coma. To give the body time to fight the infection.

They said there would likely be brain damage as the infection had caused encephalitis.

I didn't wish for death for David. But I knew that if it came it might actually be a relief.

Used to be that six thousand children a year would die from measles. In this country. Now, since the vaccine was developed in the sixties, it's one or two a year at most.

Robert   I was charged with desecrating a grave. My own mum's grave. A grave I paid for. All I was after was justice. You're the police, right? Well, I'd like to report a murder. They killed my mum! They stuck a needle in her and killed her. Now what are you going to do about it?

It only took a few weeks to convict me. The wheels of justice can spin quickly when the powers that be want them to. I got six weeks. Ha. Six weeks in jail. Because I refused to pay a fine. Well. It was five weeks but . . . I was held in contempt of court as well. For telling the judge he was corrupt, and complicit in murder.

They sent me to jail. For trying to find out the truth. How many more people have they done it to, eh? How many more people have they silenced? That's what I want to know.

There's not much to do in prison. So I had to just sit there. Thinking. About Mum. About everything.

I saw a doctor in there. Talked to him a lot. He ended up offering me meds. For depression. Trying to numb me, see. Make me compliant. I told him to fuck off. I know what he's up to. I know he's part of it all.

Part of what? He asks me. A conspiracy?

No! No! I did not say that. You don't need a conspiracy where interests converge. Conspiracy theory is a term made up to make legitimate criticism of institutions seem insane.

GP practices are given financial incentives for shifting certain types of medication. In line with the interests of the government. Did you know that? Did you? It's true. Look it up.

Mary   He has brain damage. And he lost his sight.

David.

And I have to live with that.

She composes herself.

It was in *The Lancet*. Wakefield's paper. Not the . . . *Fortean Times* for Christ's sake. It proved a link between the MMR jab and autism.

It proved it.

It was science. I say all this to my husband. Plead with him to understand. But I never apologise. Because I still think I was right. To take the risk.

Jack said he had to divorce me, on principle, but he accepted we had to stick together in the same house to look after our boys. They would have suffered the most if we had separated physically. So we only separated emotionally.

Once the boys were asleep, I'd sit in one room doing cross-stitching and drinking wine, while Jack sat in the other listening to records and drinking beer.

He would disappear some evenings. Overnight on occasion. I knew he was going on dates. I don't blame him. We're animals, right? We have our needs. Well. Most of us. I found myself just . . . numb. Living for my boys. Nothing else.

I'd drink wine and re-read the Wakefield paper. Over and over again. Like a ritual. To assure myself I had simply followed the science. I didn't understand it all. It's not my field. But I could follow enough to reassure myself. We had just been unlucky. Someone has to be.

I thought about . . .

You know. Ending things.

I thought about it. But only as a fantasy.

I imagined the peace. The nothingness.

The lack of anxiety. But I simply could not go through with it. I had to take care of my boys.

Robert   When I got out of prison I . . . I had nothing. No job. I'm not married. No kids. No parents. All my friends were online by this point so . . . I felt properly alone. Like. Properly.

I kept seeing the therapist. He asked me if I had any thoughts of hurting myself. I said of course I do. Doesn't everyone?

He said no. No they don't. Which surprised me. A lot. I just assumed everyone did.

Now and then.

Mary   One night, when Emmanuel and David were asleep upstairs, I was sitting there in my chair with my needle, and my bottle of wine, trying to get the design right on a little flower and . . .

I pricked my finger with the needle. By accident I mean, but . . .

It felt . . . I don't know.

I took the needle again and just pushed it, gently at first, underneath the fingernail of my left middle finger . . .

And I just kept pushing. Despite the pain. Or maybe because of it. Until the whole needle was under my fingernail, and blood was dripping onto my embroidery. A little blood flower.

And I felt . . .

Good. It's a weak word but it's the only one that works. Not elated. But just . . . good. For the first time in weeks. The pain was soothing. If you can believe it.

And over the weeks . . . it started becoming a regular thing. Of an evening. Until my fingernails were black.

It became my routine. Hush, little baby to both my boys. Downstairs. Wine. Stitching. Needles under my fingernails.

She laughs

Madness really. I was out of my mind. In hindsight. Really quite mad.

I got septicaemia. From the needles.

Very nearly died. Jack came to see me in hospital. Broke down apparently, when he saw me. I was unconscious. But he was there when I woke up. Holding my hand. We looked at each other and just cried. And I think he decided he had punished me enough.

It seemed like we were mending things. Me and Jack. After that. No more separate rooms in the evening. We watched TV together. We talked about what I had done. He couldn't quite forgive me but he wanted to. And he understood why I had done it. MMR vaccines were linked to autism after all. Right?

But then, a few weeks later . . . well, you know what happened don't you?

The news broke.

The Wakefield paper was a lie.

Robert *and* **Edward** *look at* **Mary**.

Scene Eight: Conclusions

Rob   The final stage of the scientific method is to reach a conclusion. To sum up your study. Or story, if you like.

Mary   Sum up? How do you sum up . . .

I mean, he made it all up. Basically. The families who took part in his study were all recruited through anti-vaccine channels. He altered facts about children's medical histories in order to support his claim. Not a single case study was accurate.

He was being paid by a law firm in America, which aimed to sue the MMR vaccine makers. He was also, at the time of his study, developing a patent for an alternative vaccine. Which would obviously have made him millions if . . . if it was taken up worldwide.

The Lancet retracted the paper. Called it utterly false.

His medical licence was revoked.

And I realised that I did what I did . . . based on lies. Fraud, to be exact.

Jack and I . . . we looked out old videos of him. Back when he was . . . capable of smiling.

We found a video of a family picnic. David was almost a year old.

He's there, on the picnic rug. Playing with cars. And you can see it. Clear as day. Two weeks before the vaccine. Zero eye contact. A lack of emotion. The frustration and violence when he can't get the little red car to run smoothly on the rug . . . It's all there. Already. Before the vaccine. We just didn't see it yet.

Signs of autism usually show up around twelve months.

The MMR vaccine is administered around twelve months.

Edward   Correlation is not causation.

Robert   You see. This is why. This is why I don't believe any of the bastards. It's just safer not to.

Mary   I found out that ten of his co-authors had disowned the study way back in 2004. Why wasn't that reported at the time? You can't run a headline saying link proven between MMR and autism and then print nothing when the authors disavow it? Can you?!

I felt like someone had stabbed me. In the heart. Just when I had come to terms . . . when Jack and I were reconciling. When I had made my peace with my decision.

I trusted him. Wakefield. I trusted the system.

Robert   This doesn't prove me wrong you know, Rob. About the Covid vaccine.

All it does is show that people in power can't be trusted.

My therapist keeps telling me trust is important. We can't live without trust. I won't be happy ever again unless I learn how to trust. I'll never be able to relax without it.

Relax. Ha.

He means comply. Stop asking awkward questions.

You do your little play. Let your audience nod along. Laugh at me, feel superior. I don't care.

Cos I've got a purpose now. I might have lost everything else but at least I know what I'm meant to do with my life.

Fight them. Expose them.

I've got a channel. YouTube. Truth Unlimited. Check it out. Three hundred subscribers in the first month. Growing every day. Every day.

I'll build that up. Get support. Maybe get on the local council. Parliament one day, who knows. Bring them down from the inside.

You watch. I'm not going away.

I'm not most people.

And I will never fucking relax. Not while the world is so blatantly corrupt.

There.

There's my conclusion.

Mary   I don't blame people who don't trust anyone. Who don't trust the police, or doctors, or scientists. Because there are people like Wakefield.

Being sceptical is good. Especially of authority.

Edward   Well, authority was sceptical of me!

Some just dismissed me as a peculiar country doctor who carried around a vial of pus with him wherever he went.

Some were afraid of losing their livelihoods.

Some could not grasp the science.

And some had built their entire identities around their beliefs and ideologies and so to change their mind would be to lose their entire sense of self.

Yes, scepticism is good but . . .

Being sceptical of everything, all the time, believing nothing anyone says, is just as foolish as believing everything they say.

One must be open minded. But not so much that one's brain falls out.

How's that for a conclusion?

Pause.

Mary   It was all already in there, you know. In my head. The doubts. About authority. Medicine. Big Pharma. All I had heard since I was young.

I wanted to believe it.

That's the truth.

These diseases, measles, rubella, smallpox – they've been around since prehistory. Mummies have been found with symptoms you know.

The diseases that survive can't be too deadly – or else they'd wipe us all out and have nothing to live on. But they can't be too mild either, or our immune system would just kill them instantly.

Just like us. We can't be too doubtful or too trusting. Too deadly or too weak. In order to survive we all have to find the right balance.

And, to conclude, some of us just can't.

They all look at each other.

Rob   Well. I think I've got everything I need so . . .

Thank you. Thank you so much for being so . . .

Thank you.

He turns off the voice recorder.

They start preparing up to leave.

Rob *approaches* **Mary**.

Rob   Do you regret it? Having kids. After all that's happened to them?

Pause.

Mary   I was so fixated on making sure David didn't turn out like Emmanuel that I forgot something so vital . . .

There's nothing *wrong* with Emmanuel. Not really. He isn't broken. He's different. He's wonderful. In so many ways. And he's growing and learning all the time, just like we all are. Without his autism he wouldn't be him. And that would be a great loss to us. To the world.

David . . . that's different. I did that to him. And I'll never forgive myself. But I don't regret having him. As a parent, Rob, no matter how things turn out, you never regret having them.

Trust me. It's worth the risk.

Pause. **Rob** *nods.* **Mary** *leaves.*

Robert *is about to leave too when he has a thought.*

Robert   Do you have kids, Rob?

Pause.

Rob   One. A girl. Mary.

Robert   How old is she?

Rob   She's ten.

Robert   And did you give Mary the Covid jab?

Pause.

Rob   Yes. We did.

Robert And she was OK?

Rob *nods his head.*

Robert   I'm glad.

He turns to leave.

Rob   She died of Covid. My mum.

Silence. **Robert** *stops. Turns back.*

Rob   Myocarditis. Caused by the virus.

It was right at the beginning, before the vaccines and . . . you know we were meant to, eh . . . shield . . . especially the elderly and . . .

But she didn't care. She was so . . . she just didn't trust that it was as bad as the government, the media, were making out.

And, to be honest . . . neither did I. I mean, all day, every day, all we get is exaggeration and outright lies. Climate change, yeah, I believe it's happening, but the number of times I've been told we only have a year or a month or a week left to save the planet . . . it becomes a bit like those doomsday cults who keep predicting the end of the world and you know, no one ever believes them.

Robert   Did you know that the manufacture of electric cars causes more harm to the environment than normal cars?

Rob   Yes. See! It's like, nothing is totally true, when you really look into it.

I mean, the number of killer diseases that were 'coming our way' long before Covid. Bird Flu. Zika. Ebola. You get . . . desensitised. Until you end up not believing a thing. Not trusting anyone. Apart from those close to you. Or maybe those telling you things you want to hear. Comforting things like . . . it's not really that bad. We don't actually need vaccines. Everything's going to be fine.

My mum said everything would be fine so . . .

I let her come visit me. In my house. During lockdown.

And . . .

She must have caught it from me, because she didn't see anyone else. I thought I just had a bit of a cold. It was nothing. It didn't really hit me hard at all but . . .

For her . . .

It wasn't nothing. It was really, really, seriously bad.

And it killed her.

I killed her.

Robert   Just like me.

Rob   No. I mean, your mum might have died from vaccine complications. She might have but . . . you were right to push her to get it.

You did the right thing and just . . . got unlucky.

Robert *stares at him.*

Robert   Thanks. But that's bullshit. If I told my mum not to get that jab she'd still be alive today.

He holds out his hand. **Rob** *shakes it.*

Robert   Truth Unlimited, yeah?

Rob *nods.* **Robert** *leaves.*

Edward *comes forwards.*

Edward   I am sorry. About your mother.

Rob   Thanks.

Edward   Mine passed when I was five. Barely remember her.

Pause. **Edward** *looks out at the audience.*

So. Did you get your answer?

Rob   What answer?

Edward   How do you know who to trust?

Rob   I don't think you ever can, for sure.

Edward   May I offer a suggestion? A direct quote from my hearing with the Royal Society of Medicine.

Rob   Sure.

Pause.

Edward *comes forth. Addresses the room.*

On the continued and sustained doubts surrounding my findings regarding vaccination against smallpox . . .

There will always be the zealots on both sides. Those men of science who are so pompous, or influenced by the promise of riches, as to ignore evidence and decry any criticism of their methods and teachings as the ignorant babble of the conspiracy addled blockhead. And, on the other side, those very blockheads who would rather seize upon the conspiracy of the day in order to feel powerful and righteous, regardless of the veracity of the claim they defend, than to step into the middle ground and engage in the difficult and murky world of the honest and open exchange of ideas.

We should trust neither of them.

These extremists will always exist. On both sides. And in many ways, they are the real victims, because they are not looking for the truth, they have only convinced themselves they are, but do nothing to demonstrate the fact.

We must take comfort in the fact that, although it may not seem it, for the extreme voices tend also to be the loudest, we, in the middle, who genuinely strive for a fair exchange of ideas, in search of the truth, those of us with quiet, honest voices, are in the majority.

We are. And we shall win. By continuing to test. By continuing to talk. We shall never silence the extremists, nor should we try to, for it is in listening to them, allowing them to speak, that we can remind ourselves of what zealotry is, where it exists, and what it is we must aim our sights away from.

Let them shout. While we think.

For the only person you should truly trust is the person who admits freely, they do not know.

Edward *takes out his violin. Plays.*

Rob, **Robert** and **Mary** *come forwards, as if entranced by the song.*

The lights come down. A perfect ending.

Until . . .

Robert   Hang on.

Jenner *scratches a string.*

And the lights snap back up. The play is not over. Apparently.

Are you calling my character a zealot?

Edward   Well . . . isn't he?

Robert   If the vaccine really killed his mum then no. He's just . . . right.

Mary   Mary didn't seize on the conspiracy of the day. She believed a scientific paper.

Rob   It's just a quote. From Jenner's work. It's not meant to directly accuse Robert or Mary of anything.

Mary   Why does he get the last word anyway?

Rob   Well he is the father of vaccination.

Mary   Bollocks is he. The whole story is a lie. Inoculation was used in China in the sixteenth century. Africa in the 1700s.

Edward   Yes but Jenner popularised it and . . .

Mary   No. No. In 1768, a doctor called John Fewster
noticed that a farmer didn't show any ill effects from
variolation treatment. The farmer said he had recently had
cowpox. Fewster made the link and discussed it at a meeting
of local doctors, one of whom attended with his nineteen
year old apprentice, who went by the name of . . .

Robert   Edward Jenner.

Edward   Good lord.

Robert   He stole it. Took all the credit.

Rob   Not exactly.

They all look at **Rob**.

Jenner's biographer made up the milkmaid thing after
Jenner's death. Cut Fewster out of the story.

Edward   Why?

Rob   To sell books, I'd guess.

Robert   So you knew it was a load of bollocks?

Rob   I only found out after draft three and by that point . . .

Rob *trails off. Shrugs*.

Robert   So what else is made up then?

Rob   It's just the Jenner stuff. The rest is verbatim.

Mary   Really? Totally verbatim.

Rob   Yes.

Mary   You really met with Mary?

Robert   And Robert?

Rob   Yup.

Mary   Interviewed them?

Robert   And used their words?

Rob   I did.

Pause.

Robert   Did your mum die of Covid?

Rob *hesitates.*

Rob   Yes.

Robert   You sure about that?

Rob *nods.*

They all look at him. Is he telling the truth?

Edward   Well, I suppose we have to believe him. He is the author. The authority.

*A strange, suspicious silence. They all continue to look at **Rob**. The whole theatre does.*

He squirms.

Rob   Right. So. Play us out Edward.

Edward   I don't /

Suddenly menacing.

Rob   / Play us out.

Edward *obeys. Begins to play.* **Rob** *looks at **Mary**. Points out front. She obeys, looks into the audience.* **Rob** *does the same to **Robert**. He reluctantly obeys too.*

*They all look out at the audience as **Edward** plays and the lights fade to black.*